This edition published in 1993 by Mimosa Books, distributed by Outlet Book Company, Inc., a Random House Company, 40 Engelhard Avenue, Avenel, New Jersey 07001.

10 9 8 7 6 5 4 3 2 1

First published in the U.K. in 1986 by Kingfisher Books

First published in the United States in 1986

Copyright © Grisewood & Dempsey Ltd. 1986

ISBN 1 85698 514 8

Printed and bound in Italy

For permission to reproduce copyright material acknowledgement and thanks are due to the following: Curtis Brown for *December* from 'The Shepherd's Calendar' by John Clare. © Copyright Eric Robinson 1964. Reproduced by permission of Curtis Brown London.

Faber and Faber for *Christmas is Coming* from 'The Country Child' by Alison Uttley. J & W Chester/ Edition Wilhelm Hansen London Limited for their arrangements of *We Three Kings, O Come All Ye Faithful* and *Away in a Manger* from 'A Feast of Easy Carols' by Carol Barratt © Copyright for all countries 1979 J & W Chester/Edition Wilhelm Hansen London Limited. Dr Frank L. Gilbert for *Winkle and the Christmas Tree* from 'Lucky Dip' (first published 1961) by Ruth Ainsworth. David Higham Associates and Chatto & Windus for *Snowflakes* from 'An English Year' by Clive Sansom. Faber & Faber and Harcourt Brace Jovanovich, Inc. for *Journey of the Magi*, reprinted by permission of Faber & Faber from 'Collected Poems 1909–1962' by T.S. Eliot; copyright 1936 Harcourt Brace Jovanovich, Inc.; © 1963, 1964 T.S. Eliot, reprinted by permission of the publisher. David Higham Associates and Macmillan for *Mary's Song* from 'Collected Poems' by Charles Causley. Oxford University Press for their arrangement of *Hark the Herald Angels Sing* from 'Christmas Carols'. (© 1985 Oxford University Press). Liveright Publishing Corporation for *little tree* from 'Tulips and Chimneys' by e e cummings (approved by Liveright Publishing Corporation) and Grafton Books, a Division of the Collins Publishing Group, for *little tree* from 'The Complete Poems 1913–1962' by e e cummings.

THE CHRISTMAS TREASURY

A COLLECTION OF STORIES, POEMS, CAROLS AND TRADITIONS

Illustrated by Jenny Thorne, Julia Rowntree
and Annabel Spenceley

MIMOSA
·BOOKS·

NEW YORK · AVENEL, NEW JERSEY

CONTENTS

CHRISTMAS IS COMING

ALISON UTTLEY

At Christmas the wind ceased to moan. Snow lay thick on the fields and the woods cast blue shadows across it. The fir trees were like sparkling, gem-laden Christmas trees, the only ones Susan had ever seen. The orchard, with the lacy old boughs outlined with snow, was a grove of fairy trees. The woods were enchanted, exquisite, the trees were holy, and anything harmful had shrunken to a thin wisp and had retreated into the depths.

The fields lay with their unevenness gone and paths obliterated, smooth white slopes criss-crossed by black lines running up to the woods. More than ever the farm seemed under a spell, like a toy in the forest, with little wooden animals and men; a brown horse led by a stiff little red-scarfed man to a yellow stable door; round, white, woolly sheep clustering round a blue trough of orange mangels; red cows drinking from a square, white trough, and returning to a painted cow-house.

Footprints were everywhere on the snow, rabbits and foxes, blackbirds, pheasants and partridges, trails of small paws, the mark of a brush, and the long feet of the cock pheasant and the tip-mark of his tail.

A jay flew out of the wood like a blue flashing diamond and came to the grass-plot for bread. A robin entered the house and hopped under the table while Susan sat very still and her father sprinkled crumbs on the floor.

Rats crouched outside the window, peeping out of the walls with gleaming eyes, seizing the birds' crumbs and scraps, and slowly lolloping back again.

Red squirrels ran along the walls to the back door, close to the window, to eat the crumbs on the bench where the milk cans froze. Every wild animal felt that a truce had come with the snow, and they visited the house where there was food in plenty, and sat with paws uplifted and noses twitching.

For the granaries were full, it had been a prosperous year, and there was food for everyone. Not like the year before when there was so little hay that Mr. Garland had to buy a stack in February. Three large haystacks as big as houses stood in the stackyard, thatched evenly and straight by Job Fletcher, who was the best thatcher for many a mile. Great mounds showed where the roots were buried. The brick-lined pit was filled with grains and in the barns were stores of corn.

The old brew-house was full of logs of wood, piled high against the walls, cut from trees which the wind had blown down. The coal-house with its strong ivied walls, part of the old fortress, had been stored with coal brought many a mile in the blaze of summer; twenty tons lay under the snow.

On the kitchen walls hung the sides of bacon and from hooks in the ceiling dangled great hams and shoulders. Bunches of onions were twisted in the pantry and barn, and an empty cow-house was stored with potatoes for immediate use.

The floor of the apple chamber was covered with apples, rosy apples, little yellow ones, like cowslip balls, wizenedy apples with withered, wrinkled cheeks, fat, well-fed smooth-faced apples, and immense green cookers, pointed like a house, which would burst in the oven and pour out a thick cream of the very essence of apples.

Even the cheese chamber had its cheeses this year, for there had been too much milk for the milkman, and the cheese presses had been put into use again. Some of them were Christmas cheeses, with layers of sage running through the middles like green ribbons.

Stone jars like those in which the forty thieves hid stood on the pantry floor, filled with white lard, and balls of fat tied up in bladders hung from the hooks. Along the broad shelves round the walls were pots of jam, blackberry and apple, from the woods and orchard, Victoria plum from the trees on house and barn, black currant from the garden, and red currant jelly, damson cheese from the half-wild ancient trees which grew everywhere, leaning over walls, dropping their blue fruit on paths and walls, in pigsty and orchard, in field and water trough, so that Susan thought they were wild as hips and haws.

Pickles and spices filled old brown pots decorated with crosses and flowers, like the pitchers and crocks of Will Shakespeare's time.

In the little dark wine chamber under the stairs were bottles of elderberry wine, purple, thick, and sweet, and golden cowslip wine, and hot ginger, some of them many years old, waiting for the winter festivities.

There were dishes piled with mince pies on the shelves of the larder, a row of plum puddings with their white calico caps, strings of sausages, and round pats of butter, with swans and cows and wheat-ears printed upon them.

Everyone who called at the farm had to eat and drink at Christmas-tide.

A few days before Christmas Mr. Garland and Dan took a bill-hook and knife and went into the woods to cut branches of scarlet-berried holly. They tied them together with ropes and dragged them down over the fields to the barn. Mr. Garland cut a bough of mistletoe from the ancient hollow hawthorn which leaned over the wall by the orchard, and thick clumps of dark-berried ivy from the walls.

Indoors, Mrs. Garland and Susan and Becky polished and rubbed and cleaned the furniture and brasses, so that everything glowed and glittered. They decorated every room, from the kitchen where every lustre jug had its sprig in its mouth, every brass candlestick had its chaplet, every copper saucepan and preserving-pan had its wreath of shining berries and leaves, through the hall, which was a bower of green, to the two parlours which were festooned and hung with holly and boughs of fir, and ivy berries dipped in red raddle, left over from sheep marking.

Holly decked every picture and ornament. Sprays hung over the bacon and twisted round the hams and herb bunches. The clock carried a crown on his head, and every dish-cover had a little sprig. Susan kept an eye on the lonely

forgotten humble things, the jelly moulds and colanders and nutmeg-graters, and made them happy with glossy leaves. Everything seemed to speak, to ask for its morsel of greenery, and she tried to leave out nothing.

On Christmas Eve fires blazed in the kitchen and parlour and even in the bedrooms. Becky ran from room to room with the red-hot salamander which she stuck between the bars to make a blaze, and Mrs. Garland took the copper warming-pan filled with glowing cinders from the kitchen fire and rubbed it between the sheets of all the beds. Susan had come down to her cosy tiny room with thick curtains at the window, and a fire in the big fireplace. Flames roared up the chimneys as Dan carried in the logs and Becky piled them on the blaze. The wind came back and tried to get in, howling at the key-holes, but all the shutters were cottered and the doors shut. The horses and mares stood in the stables, warm and happy, with nodding heads. The cows slept in the cow-houses, the sheep in the open sheds. Only Rover stood at the door of his kennel, staring up at the sky, howling to the dog in the moon, and then he, too, turned and lay down in his straw.

In the middle of the kitchen ceiling there hung the kissing-bunch, the best and brightest pieces of holly made in the shape of a large ball which dangled from the hook. Silver and gilt drops, crimson bells, blue glass trumpets, bright oranges and red polished apples, peeped and glittered through the glossy leaves. Little flags of all nations, but chiefly Turkish for some unknown reason, stuck out like quills on a hedgehog. The lamp hung near, and every little berry, every leaf, every pretty ball and apple had a tiny yellow flame reflected in its heart.

Twisted candles hung down, yellow, red, and blue, unlighted but gay, and on either side was a string of paper lanterns.

Mrs. Garland climbed on a stool and nailed on the wall the Christmas texts, "God bless our Home," "God is Love," "Peace be on this House," "A Happy Christmas and a Bright New Year."

So the preparations were made. Susan hung up her stocking at the foot of the bed and fell asleep. But soon singing roused her and she sat, bewildered. Yes, it was the carol-singers.

Outside under the stars she could see the group of men and women, with lanterns throwing beams across the paths and on to the stable door. One man stood apart beating time, another played a fiddle and another had a flute. The rest sang in four parts the Christmas hymns, "While Shepherds watched," "O come, all ye faithful," and "Hark the herald angels sing."

There was the Star, Susan could see it twinkling and bright in the dark boughs with their white frosted layers; and there was the stable. In a few hours it would be Christmas Day, the best day of all the year.

from *The Country Child*

DECEMBER

from *The Shepherd's Calendar*

While snows the window-panes bedim,
   The fire curls up a sunny charm,
Where, creaming o'er the pitcher's rim,
   The flowering ale is set to warm;
Mirth, full of joy as summer bees,
   Sits there, its pleasures to impart,
And children, 'tween their parents' knees,
   Sing scraps of carols o'er by heart.

And some, to view the winter weathers,
　　Climb up the window-seat with glee,
Likening the snow to falling feathers,
　　In fancy's infant ecstasy;
Laughing, with superstitious love,
　　O'er visions wild that youth supplies,
Of people pulling geese above,
　　And keeping Christmas in the skies.

　　　　　As tho' the homestead trees were drest,
　　　　　　In lieu of snow, with dancing leaves,
　　　　　As tho' the sun-dried martin's nest,
　　　　　　Instead of ickles, hung the eaves,
　　　　　The children hail the happy day—
　　　　　　As if the snow were April's grass,
　　　　　And pleas'd, as 'neath the warmth of May,
　　　　　　Sport o'er the water froze to glass.

John Clare

WINTER

The frost is here,
The fuel is dear,
And woods are sear,
And fires burn clear,
And frost is here
And has bitten the heel of the going year.

Bite, frost, bite!
You roll up away from the light,
The blue wood-louse, and the plump dormouse,
And the bees are stilled, and the flies are killed,
And you bite far into the heart of the house,
But not into mine.

Bite, frost, bite!
The woods are all the searer,
The fuel is all the dearer,
The fires are all the clearer,
My spring is all the nearer,
You have bitten into the heart of the earth,
But not into mine.

Alfred Lord Tennyson

WE WISH YOU A MERRY CHRISTMAS

English Carol

We wish you a Merry Christmas,
   We wish you a Merry Christmas,
We wish you a Merry Christmas
   And a Happy New Year!

Glad tidings we bring
To you and your kin.
We wish you a Merry Christmas,
And a Happy New Year.

Oh, bring us some figgy pudding,
   Oh, bring us some figgy pudding,
Oh, bring us some figgy pudding
   And a glass of good cheer!

We won't go until we get some,
   We won't go until we get some,
We won't go until we get some
   So bring it right here!

We wish you a Merry Christmas,
   We wish you a Merry Christmas,
We wish you a Merry Christmas
   And a Happy New Year!

O CHRISTMAS TREE

German Carol

1 O Christmas Tree, O Christmas Tree,
　　With lush green boughs unchanging—
　Green when the summer sun is bright,
　　And when the forest's cold and white.
　O Christmas Tree, O Christmas Tree,
　　With lush green boughs unchanging!

2 O Christmas Tree, O Christmas Tree,
　　Here once again to awe us,
　You bear round fruits of Christmas past,
　　Spun out of silver, gold, and glass.

3 O Christmas Tree, O Christmas Tree,
　　We gladly bid you welcome.
　A pyramid of light you seem,
　　A galaxy of stars that gleam.

4 O Christmas Tree, O Christmas Tree,
　　You fill the air with fragrance.
　You shrink to very tiny size,
　　Reflected in the children's eyes.

5 O Christmas Tree, O Christmas Tree,
　　What presents do you shelter?
　Rich wrappings hide the gifts from sight,
　　Done up in bows and ribbons tight.

6 O Christmas Tree, O Christmas Tree,
　　Your green limbs teach a lesson:
　That constancy and faithful cheer
　　Are gifts to cherish all the year.

18

ON THE ICE

CHARLES DICKENS

ow," said Wardle, after a substantial lunch, with the agreeable items of strong-beer and cherry-brandy, had been done ample justice to; "what say you to an hour on the ice? We shall have plenty of time."

"Capital!" said Mr. Benjamin Allen.

"Prime!" ejaculated Mr. Bob Sawyer.

"You skate, of course, Winkle?" said Wardle.

"Ye-yes; oh, yes," replied Mr. Winkle. "I—I—am *rather* out of practice."

"Oh, *do* skate, Mr. Winkle," said Arabella. "I like to see it so much."

"Oh, it is *so* graceful," said another young lady.

A third young lady said it was elegant, and a fourth expressed her opinion that it was "swan-like."

"I should be very happy, I'm sure," said Mr. Winkle, reddening; "but I have no skates."

This objection was at once overruled. Trundle had a couple of pair, and the fat boy announced that there were half-a-dozen more downstairs; whereat Mr. Winkle expressed exquisite delight, and looked exquisitely uncomfortable.

Old Wardle led the way to a pretty large sheet of ice; and the fat boy and Mr. Weller, having shovelled and swept away the snow which had fallen on it during the night, Mr. Bob Sawyer adjusted his skates with a dexterity which to Mr. Winkle was perfectly marvellous, and described circles with his left leg, and cut figures of eight, and inscribed upon the ice, without once stopping for breath, a great many other pleasant and astonishing devices, to the excessive satisfaction of Mr. Pickwick, Mr. Tupman, and the ladies: which reached a pitch of positive enthusiasm, when old Wardle and Benjamin Allen, assisted by the aforesaid Bob Sawyer, performed some mystic evolutions, which they called a reel.

All this time, Mr. Winkle, with his face and hands blue with the cold, had been forcing a gimlet into the soles of his feet, and putting his skates on, with

the points behind, and getting the straps into a very complicated and entangled state, with the assistance of Mr. Snodgrass, who knew rather less about skates than a Hindoo. At length, however, with the assistance of Mr. Weller, the unfortunate skates were firmly screwed and buckled on, and Mr. Winkle was raised to his feet.

"Now, then, sir," said Sam, in an encouraging tone; "off vith you, and show 'em how to do it."

"Stop, Sam, stop!" said Mr. Winkle, trembling violently, and clutching hold of Sam's arms with the grasp of a drowning man. "How slippery it is, Sam!"

"Not an uncommon thing upon ice, sir," replied Mr. Weller. "Hold up, sir!"

This last observation of Mr. Weller's bore reference to a demonstration Mr. Winkle made at the instant, of a frantic desire to throw his feet in the air, and dash the back of his head on the ice.

"These—these—are very awkward skates; ain't they, Sam?" inquired Mr. Winkle, staggering.

"I'm afeerd there's a orkard gen'l'm'n in 'em, sir," replied Sam.

"Now, Winkle," cried Mr. Pickwick, quite unconscious that there was anything the matter. "Come; the ladies are all anxiety."

"Yes, yes," replied Mr. Winkle, with a ghastly smile; "I'm coming."

"Just a-goin' to begin," said Sam, endeavouring to disengage himself.

"Stop an instant, Sam," gasped Mr. Winkle, clinging most affectionately to Mr. Weller. "I find I've got a couple of coats at home that I don't want, Sam. You may have them, Sam."

"Thank'ee, sir," replied Mr. Weller.

"Never mind touching your hat, Sam," said Mr. Winkle, hastily; "you needn't take your hand away to do that. I meant to have given you five shillings this morning for a Christmas box, Sam. I'll give it you this afternoon, Sam."

"You're wery good, sir," replied Mr. Weller.

"Just hold me at first, Sam; will you?" said Mr. Winkle. "There—that's right. I shall soon get in the way of it, Sam. Not too fast, Sam; not too fast."

Mr. Winkle, stooping forward with his body half doubled up, was being assisted over the ice by Mr. Weller, in a very singular and un-swanlike manner, when Mr. Pickwick most innocently shouted from the opposite bank:

"Sam!"

"Sir?" said Mr. Weller.

"Here. I want you."

"Let go, sir," said Sam. "Don't you hear the governor a-callin'? Let go, sir."

With a violent effort, Mr. Weller disengaged himself from the grasp of the agonized Pickwickian, and in so doing administered a considerable impetus to the unhappy Mr. Winkle. With an accuracy which no degree of dexterity or practice could have insured, that unfortunate gentleman bore swiftly down into the center of the reel, at the very moment when Mr. Bob Sawyer was performing a flourish of unparalleled beauty. Mr. Winkle struck wildly against him, and with a loud crash they both fell heavily down. Mr. Pickwick ran to the spot. Bob Sawyer had risen to his feet, but Mr. Winkle was far too wise to do anything of the kind, in skates. He was seated on the ice, making

spasmodic efforts to smile; but anguish was depicted on every lineament of his countenance.

"Are you hurt?" inquired Mr. Benjamin Allen, with great anxiety.

"Not much," said Mr. Winkle, rubbing his back very hard.

"I wish you'd let me bleed you," said Mr. Benjamin, with great eagerness.

"No, thank you," replied Mr. Winkle, hurriedly.

"I really think you had better," said Allen.

"Thank you," replied Mr. Winkle, "I'd rather not."

"What do *you* think, Mr. Pickwick?" inquired Bob Sawyer.

Mr. Pickwick was excited and indignant. He beckoned to Mr. Weller, and said, in a stern voice, "Take his skates off."

"No; but really I had scarcely begun," remonstrated Mr. Winkle.

"Take his skates off," repeated Mr. Pickwick firmly.

The command was not to be resisted. Mr. Winkle allowed Sam to obey in silence.

"Lift him up," said Mr. Pickwick. Sam assisted him to rise.

Mr. Pickwick retired a few paces apart from the by-standers, and, beckoning his friend to approach, fixed a searching look upon him, and uttered in a low, but distinct and emphatic tone, these remarkable words:

"You're a humbug, sir."

"A what?" said Mr. Winkle, starting.

"A humbug, sir. I will speak plainer, if you wish it. An impostor, sir."

With those words Mr. Pickwick turned slowly on his heel, and rejoined his friends.

While Mr. Pickwick was delivering himself of the sentiment just recorded, Mr. Weller and the fat boy, having by their joint endeavours cut out a slide, were exercising themselves thereupon in a very masterly and brilliant manner. Sam Weller, in particular, was displaying that beautiful feat of fancy sliding which is currently denominated "knocking at the cobbler's door," and which is achieved by skimming over the ice on one foot, and occasionally giving a postman's knock upon it with the other. It was a good long slide, and there was something in the motion which Mr. Pickwick, who was very cold with standing still, could not help envying.

"It looks nice warm exercise that, doesn't it?" he inquired of Wardle, when that gentleman was thoroughly out of breath by reason of the indefatigable manner in which he had converted his legs into a pair of compasses, and drawn complicated problems on the ice.

"Ah, it does indeed," replied Wardle. "Do you slide?"

"I used to do so, on the gutters, when I was a boy," replied Mr. Pickwick.

"Try it now," said Wardle.

"Oh, do, please, Mr. Pickwick!" cried all the ladies.

"I should be very happy to afford you any amusement," replied Mr. Pickwick, "but I haven't done such a thing these thirty years."

"Pooh! pooh! Nonsense!" said Wardle, dragging off his skates with the impetuosity which characterized all his proceedings. "Here; I'll keep you company; come along!" And away went the good tempered old fellow down the slide, with a rapidity which came very close upon Mr. Weller, and beat the fat boy all to nothing.

Mr. Pickwick paused, considered, pulled off his gloves and put them in his hat; took two or three short runs, balked himself as often, and at last took another run, and went slowly and gravely down the slide, with his feet about a yard and a quarter apart, amidst the gratified shouts of all the spectators.

"Keep the pot a-bilin', sir!" said Sam; and down went Wardle again, and then Mr. Pickwick, and then Sam, and then Mr. Winkle, and then Mr. Bob Sawyer, and then the fat boy, and then Mr. Snodgrass, following closely upon each other's heels, and running after each other with as much eagerness as if all their future prospects in life depended on their expedition.

It was the most intensely interesting thing, to observe the manner in which Mr. Pickwick performed his share in the ceremony; to watch the torture of anxiety with which he viewed the person behind, gaining upon him at the imminent hazard of tripping him up; to see him gradually expend the painful force which he had put on at first, and turn slowly round on the slide, with his face towards the point from which he had started; to contemplate the playful smile which mantled on his face when he had accomplished the distance, and the eagerness with which he turned round when he had done so and ran after his predecessor; his black gaiters tripping pleasantly through the snow, and his eyes beaming cheerfulness and gladness through his spectacles. And when he was knocked down (which happened upon the average every third round), it was the most invigorating sight that can possibly be imagined, to behold him gather up his hat, gloves, and handkerchief, with a glowing countenance, and resume his station in the rank, with an ardour and enthusiasm that nothing could abate.

The sport was at its height, the sliding was at the quickest, the laughter was at the loudest, when a sharp smart crack was heard. There was a quick rush towards the bank, a wild scream from the ladies, and a shout from Mr. Tupman. A large mass of ice disappeared; the water bubbled up over it; Mr. Pickwick's hat, gloves, and handkerchief were floating on the surface; and this was all of Mr. Pickwick that anybody could see.

Dismay and anguish were depicted on every countenance; the males turned pale, and the females fainted; Mr. Snodgrass and Mr. Winkle grasped each other by the hand, and gazed at the spot where their leader had gone down, with frenzied eagerness; while Mr. Tupman, by way of rendering the promptest assistance, and at the same time conveying to any persons who might be within hearing, the clearest possible notion of the catastrophe, ran off across the country at his utmost speed, screaming "Fire!" with all his might.

It was at this moment, when old Wardle and Sam Weller were approaching the hole with cautious steps, and Mr. Benjamin Allen was holding a hurried consultation with Mr. Bob Sawyer on the advisability of bleeding the company generally, as an improving little bit of professional practice—it was

at this very moment that a face, head, and shoulders emerged from beneath the water, and disclosed the features and spectacles of Mr. Pickwick.

"Keep yourself up for an instant—for only one instant!" bawled Mr. Snodgrass.

"Yes, do; let me implore you—for my sake!" roared Mr. Winkle, deeply affected. The adjuration was rather unnecessary; the probability being that if Mr. Pickwick had declined to keep himself up for anybody else's sake, it would have occurred to him that he might as well do so for his own.

"Do you feel the bottom there, old fellow?" said Wardle.

"Yes, certainly," replied Mr. Pickwick, wringing the water from his head and face, and gasping for breath. "I fell upon my back. I couldn't get on my feet at first."

The clay upon so much of Mr. Pickwick's coat as was yet visible bore testimony to the accuracy of this statement; and as the fears of the spectators were still further relieved by the fat boy's suddenly recollecting that the water was nowhere more than five feet deep, prodigies of valour were performed to get him out. After a vast quantity of splashing, and cracking,

and struggling, Mr. Pickwick was at length fairly extricated from his unpleasant position, and once more stood on dry land.

"Oh, he'll catch his death of cold," said Emily.

"Dear old thing!" said Arabella. "Let me wrap this shawl round you, Mr. Pickwick."

"Ah, that's the best thing you can do," said Wardle; "and when you've got it on, run home as fast as your legs can carry you, and jump into bed directly."

A dozen shawls were offered on the instant. Three or four of the thickest having been selected, Mr. Pickwick was wrapped up, and started off, under the guidance of Mr. Weller; presenting the singular phenomenon of an elderly gentleman, dripping wet, and without a hat, with his arms bound down to his sides, skimming over the ground, without any clearly defined purpose, at the rate of six good English miles an hour.

But Mr. Pickwick cared not for appearances in such an extreme case, and urged on by Sam Weller, he kept at the very top of his speed until he reached the door of Manor Farm, where Mr. Tupman had arrived some five minutes before, and had frightened the old lady into palpitations of the heart by impressing her with the unalterable conviction that the kitchen chimney was on fire—a calamity which always presented itself in glowing colours to the old lady's mind when anybody about her evinced the smallest agitation.

Mr. Pickwick paused not an instant until he was snug in bed.

from *The Pickwick Papers*

WE THREE KINGS
American Carol

We three Kings of O - ri - ent are, Bear - ing gifts we

tra-verse a - far, Field and foun - tain, moor and moun - tain,

CHORUS

Fol - low-ing yon - der star. O,_____ Star of won - der,

star of night, Star with roy - al beau - ty bright, West - ward

lead - ing, still pro - ceed - ing, Guide us to Thy per - fect light.

28

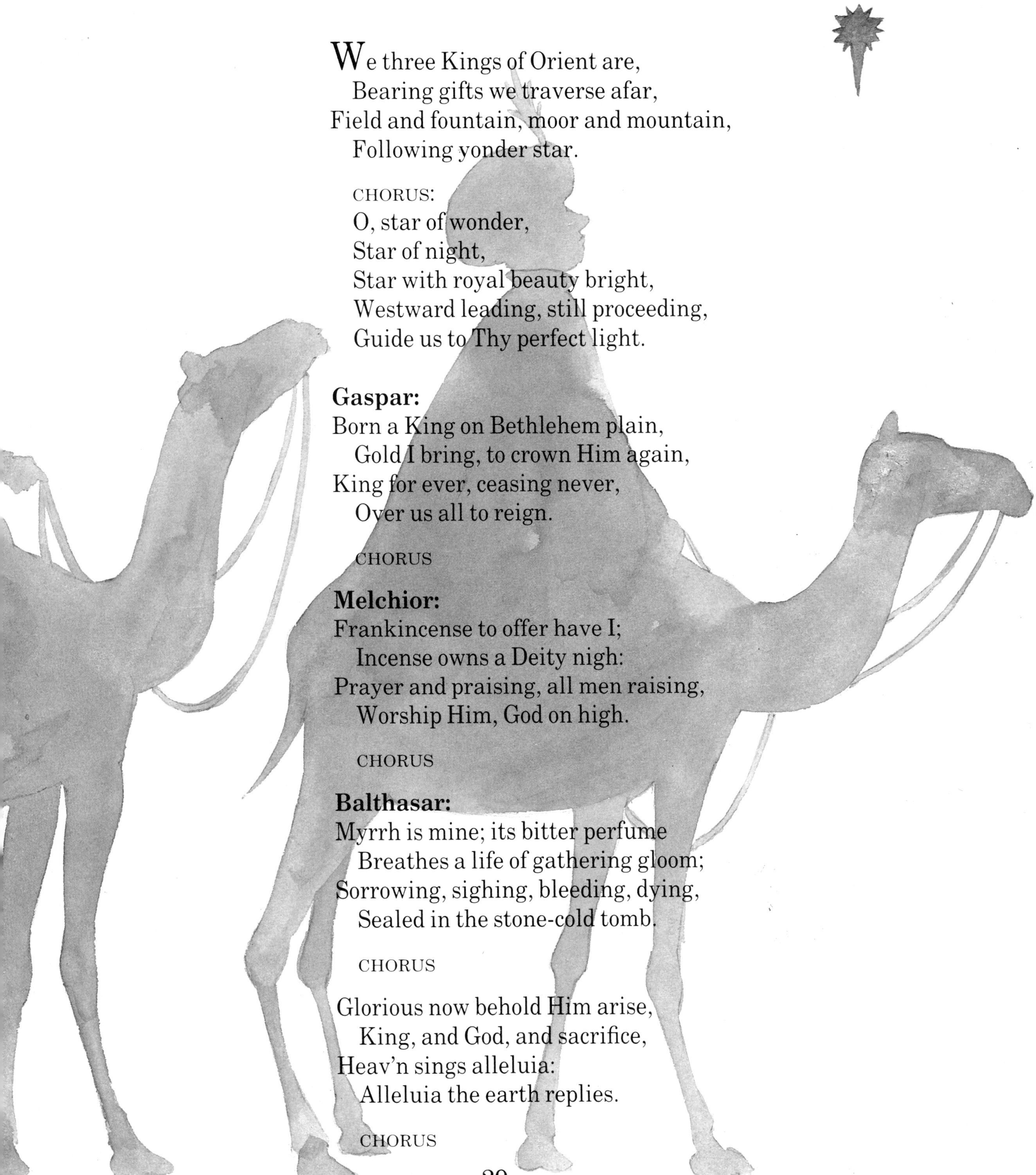

We three Kings of Orient are,
  Bearing gifts we traverse afar,
Field and fountain, moor and mountain,
  Following yonder star.

CHORUS:
  O, star of wonder,
  Star of night,
  Star with royal beauty bright,
  Westward leading, still proceeding,
  Guide us to Thy perfect light.

Gaspar:
Born a King on Bethlehem plain,
  Gold I bring, to crown Him again,
King for ever, ceasing never,
  Over us all to reign.

CHORUS

Melchior:
Frankincense to offer have I;
  Incense owns a Deity nigh:
Prayer and praising, all men raising,
  Worship Him, God on high.

CHORUS

Balthasar:
Myrrh is mine; its bitter perfume
  Breathes a life of gathering gloom;
Sorrowing, sighing, bleeding, dying,
  Sealed in the stone-cold tomb.

CHORUS

Glorious now behold Him arise,
  King, and God, and sacrifice,
Heav'n sings alleluia:
  Alleluia the earth replies.

CHORUS

29

CHRISTMAS DECORATIONS

NORA CLARKE

Christmas decorations are a mixture of old and new traditions. One of the oldest is the gathering of evergreens for the house. This has been going on since before Christianity, and was associated with very early mid-winter festivals.

Holly with its glossy leaves and shining red berries is a cheerful sight on cold wintry days and this is why we bring it inside. It reminds us that some shrubs bloom in spite of snow and frosts and that life will return to all other trees and shrubs in the spring. Holly wreaths on the front door are a sign of good luck.

Ivy too has shining leaves that cling to walls and branches whatever the weather. Ivy is a sign of friendship, remaining firm and strong for years, so it is particularly popular at Christmas when we remember our friends.

Mistletoe with its distinctive white berries grows out of apple trees in the orchard. An old tradition says that if friends meet under mistletoe they will both have good fortune, and that if enemies meet then they will stop quarreling. If you hang a spray of mistletoe in your house you can claim a kiss from anyone standing underneath it.

In the past it was traditional to strew herbs on the floor, which would give out a sweet smell. Floors do not need this nowadays, but some people still put rosemary into a vase, as rosemary is the herb for remembering friends once again.

Later on—during the reign of Queen Victoria—tinsel, garlands, candles and lights were added to evergreens as Christmas decorations. Christmas trees also became popular around this time. Christmas crackers, so familiar today, began as a pretty way of wrapping sweets. Printed mottoes and funny riddles were added by a Londoner called Tom Smith, who had first seen these little rolls of colored paper around candies on sale in Paris. But not many people bought his pretty packets at first. It was when he started to put crackers inside that the idea really caught on. He was inspired by looking into a log fire and seeing it sparkle and crackle. After much hard work he managed to think up a way of getting thin strips of cardboard to explode inside the colored wrappings. Tom Smith started the first cracker factory, and though he added tiny toys and paper hats, he insisted that every cracker must have a motto, or a joke and riddle as well.

31

WINKLE AND THE CHRISTMAS TREE

RUTH AINSWORTH

Tabby cat and her three kittens slept in a box under the kitchen table. When the kittens grew bigger and their legs became stronger, Tabby Cat sometimes took them for a walk into the dining room, or the sitting room, or the hall.

In the dining room was a gas fire which hissed and had an angry red face. Winkle, who was the bravest of the kittens, hissed back at it.

In the hall was a row of shoes and slippers. The kittens played with the shoe laces and sometimes, when they were tired, they crept into a slipper and fell asleep there because it was so warm and soft, like a cradle.

When it was almost Christmas time, a tall green Christmas tree was brought into the hall, and hung with pretty lights and glass balls and presents done up in gay paper. On the top a Fairy Doll was perched with a silver wand in her hand.

The kittens could do nothing but stare at the beautiful tree.

"May we climb it?" they asked.

"May we bite it?"

"May we lick the candles?"

"Shall we get one of those presents?" they asked.

But Mother Cat's answer to all those questions was "NO."

"You may *look*," said Tabby Cat, "and that is all. The tree is for the children, not for you. You might, if you were good, have a special present each, but you will find it beside your box when you wake up on Christmas morning."

Winkle was not content with just looking. He wanted to sniff with his little black nose, and to lick with his small pink tongue, and to touch with his furry paws. So that night, when his two sisters and Tabby Cat were all asleep, he crept softly out of the box and crossed the kitchen floor. He tiptoed into the hall, scrambled up the side of the tub in which the Christmas tree was planted, and began very carefully to climb up.

Climbing was not as nice as he had expected. The branches of the tree were springy and difficult to cling to, and the thin pointed leaves pricked his nose. His feet caught in the strings of tinsel and paper chains. But he kept on, and at last he reached the top, and found his little damp nose almost touching the golden hair and smooth pink cheeks of the Fairy Doll.

"A happy Christmas!" said the Fairy Doll. "You are the first kitten who has ever climbed our Christmas tree."

"A happy Christmas!" replied Winkle. "You are the first Fairy Doll I have ever spoken to."

"But you must get down at once, before your mother wakes up and misses you," said the Fairy Doll. "Go carefully. You might spoil something if you slipped."

Winkle went very carefully, but he had to go down head first and that made him feel very dizzy. When he was halfway down, his paws slipped away from a prickly branch. He clutched at a candle to save himself, but the wax was too smooth and slippery for him to hold. He caught at a string of tinsel for a moment—but the string broke. He leaped at a glass ball and rocked on it till it fell off the tree and smashed on the floor into a thousand splinters.

Winkle fell as well, but he landed on the soft earth inside the tub, and was not hurt.

He picked himself up, and shook himself from his ears right down to the tip of his tail. Then he looked at the broken glass ball. No one could mend it, he was sure. It had been like a lovely shining bubble of a ball. Now it lay on the floor, a thousand jagged scraps of fine glass.

Winkle looked up at the Fairy Doll and mewed sadly:

"Please help me, Fairy Doll! Please help me! Please put the broken ball together again. I know you can with your magic wand. Please try."

"I will try," said the Fairy Doll, "but I don't think I can do anything as difficult as that."

She spread her fairy wings and flew down from her high branch, and waved her silver wand over the broken glass ball.

Nothing happened.

"Try harder," mewed Winkle.

"Try harder," the Fairy Doll whispered to her wand, and she waved it twice.

Still nothing happened.

Then she gave the wand a shake and said crossly:

"You *must* try harder, *much* harder! You must make more magic. You are no better than a clothes' peg."

The magic wand did not like to be scolded, so the third time the Fairy Doll waved it, it tried very hard indeed, and the tiny glass splinters swept themselves together and made a shining glass ball again, as good as new.

"Thank you, oh, thank you," purred Winkle, as the Fairy Doll flew up and hung the glass ball in its proper place on the tree.

When the kittens woke up next morning, they found their presents lying on the kitchen rug beside their bed. There was a ping-pong ball for each of them —and what fun they were! The three ping-pong balls rolled all over the floor, and the kittens went chasing after them. Tabby Cat was kept busy hooking them out with her paw from under cupboards and inside the fender.

Winkle never tried to climb the Christmas tree again, but he always waved his tail to the Fairy Doll when he went into the hall, and she waved her wand back. And when he saw the shining glass ball, he purred to himself and thought that that was his secret—his and the Fairy Doll's.

SNOWFLAKES

And did you know
That every flake of snow
That forms so high
In the grey winter sky
And falls so far,
Is a bright six-pointed star?
Each crystal grows
A flower as perfect as a rose.
Lace could never make
The patterns of a flake.
No brooch
Of figured silver could approach
Its delicate craftsmanship. And think:
Each pattern is distinct.
Of all the snowflakes floating there—
The million million in the air—
None is the same. Each star
Is newly forged, as faces are,
Shaped to its own design
Like yours and mine.
And yet . . . each one
Melts when its flight is done;
Holds frozen loveliness
A moment, even less;
Suspends itself in time—
And passes like a rhyme.

Clive Sansom

WHILE SHEPHERDS WATCH'D

English Carol

While shepherds watch'd their flocks by night,
   All seated on the ground,
The angel of the Lord came down,
   And glory shone around.

"Fear not," said he, for mighty dread
   Had seized their troubled mind;
"Glad tidings of great joy I bring
   To you and all mankind.

"To you, in David's town, this day
   Is born of David's line
The Saviour, who is Christ the Lord;
   And this shall be the sign:

"The heav'nly Babe you there shall find
   To human view displayed,
All meanly wrapped in swathing bands,
   And in a manger laid."

Thus spake the seraph; and forthwith
   Appeared a shining throng
Of angels praising God, who thus
   Addressed their joyful song:

"All glory be to God on high
   And to the earth be peace;
Good will henceforth from heav'n to men
   Begin and never cease."

Nahum Tate

ON THE MORNING OF CHRIST'S NATIVITY

No war, or battle's sound
Was heard the world around:
The idle spear and shield were high uphung;
The hookèd chariot stood
Unstained with hostile blood;
The trumpet spake not to the armèd throng;
And kings sat still with awful eye,
As if they surely knew their sovereign Lord was by.

But peaceful was the night
Wherein the Prince of Light
His reign of peace upon the earth began:
The winds, with wonder whist,
Smoothly the waters kissed,
Whispering new joys to the mild oceàn,
Who now hath quite forgot to rave,
While birds of calm sit brooding on the charmèd wave.

John Milton

THE ORIGIN OF THE CHRISTMAS TREE

NORA CLARKE

It is hard to imagine what Christmas would be like without the Christmas trees that decorate our homes and public places. Not so long ago, though, Christmas trees were unknown in the United States and most of the rest of the world as well.

Strangely enough, the Roman soldiers who marched over Europe many centuries ago decorated pine trees during their special midwinter festival, the *Saturnalia*, which was held in honor of the god Saturn. At about that time, mainly in northern Europe, it was believed that evergreen shrubs and trees were sacred. They had to be given presents and sacrifices. The story is told that Boniface of England, an early Christian saint, was traveling in Germany telling people all about his beliefs. He rested under an oak tree where human beings had been killed as offerings to

40

the pagan gods. Boniface chopped the tree down and as the oak fell a little fir tree started to grow in its place. St. Boniface used this little tree as a symbol of his religious message.

A few years later another legend arose, also in Germany. It was said that just as cattle in the fields bowed their heads when the Christ-child was born, so trees in the forest put out green leaves. After that, evergreen branches, especially from pine trees, were carried inside houses and called Christmas trees. The evergreen trees were not decorated until about 1530 when Martin Luther, a religious leader in Germany, was walking home on a clear frosty Christmas Eve. Millions of stars twinkled down at him and he thought they were so beautiful that when he reached home he tied candles to the branches of a fir tree. Luther wanted children to see these candles shining through the dark to remind them of the stable in Bethlehem. In those days there were many forests but people did not dig up or chop down big fir trees. They just decorated

the trees where they stood outside. In the United States today, many people keep their large trees in public places or outside churches. After a time rosy apples were added to the candles tied on the trees and later very small fir trees were carried inside the house. Perhaps this was to enable children to decorate the tree. By this time flowers, lengths of ribbon, candies in pretty wrappings and candles were used as decoration.

German and Dutch people who emigrated to distant lands kept up their Christmas Tree tradition, singing the carol "O Tannenbaum" as the candles were lit. It was the German-born Prince Albert, Queen Victoria's husband, who brought the Christmas Tree to Britain. In 1841 he arranged a beautiful tree at Windsor Castle and Queen Victoria said that the royal children "are full of happy wonder at the German Christmas Tree and its radiant candles."

Everybody rushed to follow the royal example and shining ornaments and other beautiful decorations became fashionable. Candles are not used on trees nowadays for safety reasons but the electric lights in pretty shapes and glowing colors are a reminder of Martin Luther's candles over four hundred years ago.

THE FIRST NOEL

English Carol

The first Noel the angel did say
  Was to certain poor shepherds in fields as they lay;
In fields as they lay, keeping their sheep,
  In a cold winter's night that was so deep.

CHORUS:

  Noel, Noel, Noel, Noel,
  Born is the King of Israel!

They lookèd up and saw a star
  Shining in the east, beyond them far,
And to the earth it gave great light,
  And so it continued both day and night.

  CHORUS

And by the light of that same star,
  Three wise men came from country far;
To seek for a king was their intent,
  And to follow the star wherever it went.

  CHORUS

This star drew nigh to the northwest,
 O'er Bethlehem it took its rest,
And there it did both stop and stay
 Right over the place where Jesus lay.

 CHORUS

Then entered in those wise men three
 Full rev'rently upon their knee,
And offered there in his presence
 Their gold, and myrrh, and frankincense.

 CHORUS

Then let us all with one accord
 Sing praises to our heavenly Lord;
That hath made heaven and earth of naught,
 And with his blood mankind hath bought.

 CHORUS

THE CHRISTMAS STORY

NORA CLARKE

lmost two thousand years ago a young girl called Mary lived in the village of Nazareth in Palestine. One day, when she was sitting alone quietly thinking, a dazzling light suddenly flashed all around her. She was frightened but as she protected her face she heard a gentle voice calming her fears.

"Do not be afraid, Mary, for you have found favor with God."

Slowly, still fearful, she uncovered her eyes. Before her, with a halo of glory, stood a messenger from God, the angel Gabriel. This was the message that he brought:

"Behold, you will bear a son whose name shall be called Jesus. He will grow up to be called the son of God, the Savior of all people and King for ever and ever."

Mary was astonished. She did not know why such a thing had happened to her, but having faith in God, she whispered softly,

"Be it done unto me as you have said."

At these words the angel left Mary and the wondrous light dimmed.

In the same village lived Joseph, a carpenter. He too was puzzled when Mary told him of her visit from the angel Gabriel, but he loved Mary very much so he married her and promised to protect her and her baby son.

Now at that time Palestine was ruled by the Romans. One day the Roman Governor demanded that every man must pay a tax and their numbers must be counted. He ordered all men to go with their families to the town of their ancestors to register. As Joseph was a descendant of the great King David, he had to return to David's city, Bethlehem, which was several days' ride away. Mary's baby was almost due so she sat on their little donkey and Joseph trudged wearily beside her. It was a long, hard journey.

There were many other families traveling to Bethlehem to be taxed and counted and when at last Mary and Joseph reached the town it was late and they could find nowhere to stay.

"No room! Sorry, no room at this inn," people called time and again. At last, utterly exhausted, they stumbled through the town to the very last house.

"No room!" cried the innkeeper, but then he noticed Mary's pale face, and saw how weary and cold they looked. His voice softened.

"I can only offer shelter in my stable. The straw is clean though, and my ox and ass are very gentle and will keep you warm."

Mary and Joseph, greatly relieved, made their way to the stable. That night Jesus was born. He had no cradle but Mary wrapped him lovingly in swaddling clothes and laid him in a manger filled with hay. The animals breathed over the baby to keep him warm and Joseph watched over his family.

Now in a land far from Bethlehem lived three Kings whose names were Melchior, Gaspar, and Balthasar. One night they noticed a mysterious star shining in the east, brighter than any other star in the sky. They hurried to their holy books which were full of prophecy to try to discover what the star could mean. Then they spent much time thinking and talking among themselves. Finally the kings said to one another.

"Let us journey toward the star," for being wise men they felt deep inside that the star signified a very great event.

And so they gathered their provisions, mounted their camels and set out across the desert. The light of the star was their only guide and it shone more intensely as they drew nearer and nearer to Bethlehem. Finally, after journeying for twelve long days and nights, the kings were drawn to the stable where Mary and Joseph cared for their newborn child. Suddenly realizing that they were in the presence of Jesus, the son of God, the three kings dropped to their knees and bowed their heads. Feeling blessed to witness such a wondrous sight, they offered the baby their most treasured belongings—gold, frankincense, and myrrh—gold, a gift for kings, frankincense to be burned in honor of God, and myrrh, a bitter perfume for preserving the dead.

That same chilly night shepherds were guarding their sheep in the fields above Bethlehem. At first they noticed a great number of stars in the sky, and then suddenly a blinding light shone down upon them and the frightened shepherds saw an angel of God before them.

"Fear not," the angel said, "for I bring you tidings of great joy. This night Christ the Lord is born. Go to Bethlehem, the city of royal David, where you will find the baby, the Savior of the world, lying in a manger."

Then the shepherds heard choirs of angels singing the first carol:

"Glory to God in the highest

And peace to his people on earth."

The shepherds remained silent while the brilliant light faded, wondering at the angel's words. Then they turned to one another:

"Let us go and see this thing that has happened. Let us go to Bethlehem and see for ourselves the Savior of the world."

Gathering up two of their best lambs to present as gifts, they hurried away to the town. They found Mary and Joseph, just as the angel had foretold, in a stable, with the baby sleeping in a manger.

The shepherds were overjoyed that the angel's message was true and they knelt and worshiped the baby. Then they went back to their sheep, telling everyone on their way of the wonder they had seen.

THE HOLLY AND THE IVY

English Carol

1　The holly and the ivy,
　　　When they are both full grown,
　Of all the trees that are in the wood,
　　　The holly bears the crown.

　　CHORUS:
　　The rising of the sun
　　And the running of the deer,
　　The playing of the merry organ,
　　Sweet singing in the choir.

2　The holly bears a blossom
　　　As white as the lily flower,
　And Mary bore sweet Jesus Christ,
　　　To be our sweet saviour:

　　CHORUS

3　The holly bears a berry,
　　　As red as any blood,
　And Mary bore sweet Jesus Christ
　　　To do poor sinners good.

　　CHORUS

4　The holly bears a prickle,
　　　As sharp as any thorn,
　And Mary bore sweet Jesus Christ
　　　On Christmas Day in the morn.

　　CHORUS

5　The holly bears a bark,
　　　As bitter as any gall,
　And Mary bore sweet Jesus Christ
　　　For to redeem us all

　　CHORUS

6　The holly and the ivy,
　　　When they are both full grown,
　Of all the trees that are in the wood,
　　　The holly bears the crown.

　　CHORUS

THE BOAR'S HEAD CAROL

Traditional English

The boar's head in hand bear I,
   Bedecked with bays and rosemary;
And I pray you, my masters, be merry,
   Quot estis in convivio:
   Caput apri defero
   Reddens laudes Domino.

The boar's head, as I understand,
   Is the rarest dish in all the land,
When thus bedecked with a gay garland,
   Let us *servire cantico:*
   Caput apri defero,
   Reddens laudes Domino.

Our steward hath provided this,
   In honour of the King of bliss,
Which on this day to be served is,
   In Reginensi atrio:
   Caput apri defero,
   Reddens laudes Domino.

The story goes that a student of The Queen's College, Oxford, was attacked by a wild boar on Christmas Day. He killed the animal by stuffing a book down its throat, which he then retrieved by cutting off the head. He carried the head to the College's High Table, where the feast is celebrated every year.

TRANSLATION
Quot . . . So many as are in the feast.
Caput . . . The boar's head I bring, giving praises to God.
Servire . . . Let us serve with a song.
In . . . In the Queen's hall.

51

CHRISTMAS FOOD

NORA CLARKE

Most families today try to have some special food to eat on Christmas Day. Turkey, plum pudding, mince pies, nuts, Christmas cake all add up to a very large meal indeed. But our ancestors, at least the richer ones, enjoyed enormous feasts which included sides of beef, geese, turkey, partridge, swans, peacocks, every kind of fish, with a boar's head as a centerpiece. And there were very many puddings to follow. It is said that Elizabeth I greatly enjoyed trifles and Henry VIII loved marchpane, or marzipan.

Most animals which provided these feasts had to be slaughtered about mid-December because there was no way of storing sufficient roots and hay to feed them through the winter. The family pig and chickens had to be eaten once the acorns and beechnuts in the forests were finished. As this usually happened near to Christmas, perhaps a little extra meat would be set aside for a special celebration meal.

Centuries ago careful housewives tried hard to find ways of preserving food to last the household through the long winter months. They salted or dried many things, including the plums which we call prunes. These plums gave their name to the first Christmas puddings which included many fruits, suet, scraps of meat, ale, brandy, or cider. This sweet and sour mixture was shaped into balls, wrapped in white cloths, and then boiled into a solid mass. Some plum puddings were eaten at Christmas and the rest were kept until Easter.

Mince pies are a popular Christmas speciality today. When mincemeat was first made it really did contain meat. Beef, rabbit, pheasant, chicken, hare, mushrooms, spices, and vinegar were all finely chopped up

together and then baked in a large pie shaped like a manger. Our ancestors must have had enormous appetites, and stomachs too, as this pie would come to the table after all the roasts and plum pudding had been eaten and when quantities of ale had already been drunk. For in those days a warm, spiced ale was the traditional Christmas drink. Everybody would drink from a special bowl and sing or shout "wassail" (meaning "be of good health") as the bowl was handed round. Gradually housewives started to use fruit and nuts rather than meat in their puddings and cakes, partly because meat did not keep fresh for as long. Today it is only the name which reminds us of the original mincemeat recipe.

Christmas cake, which most people now take for granted, is actually quite a modern idea. It is said that Prince Albert, Queen Victoria's husband, loved rich, solid cakes. He wanted something specially baked for Christmas tea with the royal children. He asked for a plum-cake very like a modern Christmas cake mixture, with little decorations of robins, snowmen, and other wintry objects on top.

Different countries have their own traditional food, often very different from ours. The Italians have a special cake called *panetone*, which is often eaten immediately after a midnight church service. The French have a Christmas cake shaped like a yule log which is covered in thick chocolate and topped with cream, to give the effect of snow. The Norwegians bake a special bread, called *Julekake*, filled with raisins, candied peel and spices. Dutch Christmas cake is called a *banketletter*. This is made from marzipan and pastry, rolled into letters. These can be the first letter of the family name or little initials for each person present.

And finally, the Finnish have a special Christmas dinner which to us may seem rather strange. They enjoy ham, salted meat and pickled herrings, with carrots, turnips and salted cucumber.

CHRISTMAS AT THE CRATCHITS'

CHARLES DICKENS

T hen up rose Mrs. Cratchit, Cratchit's wife, dressed out but poorly in a twice-turned gown, but brave in ribbons, which are cheap and make a goodly show for sixpence; and she laid the cloth, assisted by Belinda Cratchit, second of her daughters, also brave in ribbons; while Master Peter Cratchit plunged a fork into the saucepan of potatoes, and getting the corners of his monstrous shirt collar (Bob's private property, conferred upon his son and heir in honour of the day) into his mouth, rejoiced to find himself so gallantly attired, and yearned to show his linen in the fashionable Parks. And now two smaller Cratchits, boy and girl, came tearing in, screaming that outside the baker's they had smelt the goose, and known it for their own; and basking in luxurious thoughts of sage and onion, these young Cratchits danced about the table, and exalted Master Peter Cratchit to the skies, while he (not proud, although his collars nearly choked him) blew the fire, until the slow potatoes bubbling up, knocked loudly at the saucepan lid to be let out and peeled.

"What has ever got your precious father?" said Mrs. Cratchit. "And your brother, Tiny Tim! And Martha warn't as late last Christmas Day by half-an-hour!"

"Here's Martha, Mother!" said a girl, appearing as she spoke.

"Here's Martha, Mother!" cried the two young Cratchits. "Hurrah! There's *such* a goose, Martha!"

"Why, bless your heart alive, my dear, how late you are!" said Mrs. Cratchit, kissing her a dozen times, and taking off her shawl and bonnet for her with officious zeal.

"We'd a deal of work to finish up last night," replied the girl, "and had to clear away this morning, Mother!"

"Well! Never mind so long as you are come," said Mrs. Cratchit. "Sit ye down before the fire, my dear, and have a warm, Lord bless ye!"

"No, no! There's Father coming!" cried the two young Cratchits, who were everywhere at once. "Hide, Martha, hide!"

So Martha hid herself, and in came little Bob, the father, with at least three feet of comforter exclusive of the fringe, hanging down before him; and his threadbare clothes darned up and brushed, to look seasonable; and Tiny Tim upon his shoulder. Alas for Tiny Tim, he bore a little crutch, and had his limbs supported by an iron frame!

"Why, where's our Martha?" cried Bob Cratchit, looking round.

"Not coming," said Mrs. Cratchit.

"Not coming!" said Bob, with a sudden declension in his high spirits; for he had been Tim's blood horse all the way from church, and had come home rampant. "Not coming upon Christmas Day!"

Martha didn't like to see him disappointed, if it were only in joke; so she came out prematurely from behind the closet door, and ran into his arms, while the two young Cratchits hustled Tiny Tim, and bore him off into the wash-house, that he might hear the pudding singing in the copper.

"And how did little Tim behave?" asked Mrs. Cratchit, when she had rallied Bob on his credulity, and Bob had hugged his daughter to his heart's content.

"As good as gold," said Bob, "and better. Somehow he gets thoughtful, sitting by himself so much, and thinks the strangest things you ever heard. He told me, coming home, that he hoped the people saw him in the church, because he was a cripple, and it might be pleasant to them to remember upon Christmas Day, who made lame beggars walk and blind men see."

Bob's voice was tremulous when he told them this, and trembled more when he said that Tiny Tim was growing strong and hearty.

His active little crutch was heard upon the floor, and back came Tiny Tim before another word was spoken, escorted by his brother and sister to his stool before the fire; and while Bob, turning up his cuffs—as if, poor fellow, they were capable of being made more shabby—compounded some hot mixture in a jug with gin and lemons, and stirred it round and round and put it on the hob to simmer, Master Peter and the two ubiquitous young Cratchits went to fetch the goose, with which they soon returned in high procession.

Such a bustle ensued that you might have thought a goose the rarest of all birds; a feathered phenomenon, to which a black swan was a matter of course, and in truth it was something very like it in that house. Mrs. Cratchit made the gravy (ready beforehand in a little saucepan) hissing hot; Master Peter mashed the potatoes with incredible vigour; Miss Belinda sweetened up the apple sauce; Martha dusted the hot plates; Bob took Tiny Tim beside him in a tiny corner at the table; the two young Cratchits set chairs for everybody, not forgetting themselves, and mounting guard upon their posts, crammed spoons into their mouths, lest they should shriek for goose before their turn came to be helped. At last the dishes were set on, and grace was said. It was succeeded by a breathless pause, as Mrs. Cratchit, looking slowly all along the carving-knife, prepared to plunge it in the breast; but when she did, and when the long-expected gush of stuffing issued forth, one murmur of delight arose all around the board, and even Tiny Tim, excited by the two young Cratchits, beat on the table with the handle of his knife, and feebly cried Hurrah!

There never was such a goose. Bob said he didn't believe there ever was such a goose cooked. Its tenderness and flavour, size and cheapness, were the themes of universal admiration. Eked out by the apple sauce and mashed potatoes, it was a sufficient dinner for the whole family; indeed, as Mrs. Cratchit said with great delight (surveying one small atom of a bone upon the

dish), they hadn't ate it all at last! Yet everyone had had enough, and the youngest Cratchits, in particular, were steeped in sage and onion to the eyebrows! But now, the plates being changed by Miss Belinda, Mrs. Cratchit left the room alone—too nervous to bear witnesses—to take the pudding up and bring it in.

Suppose it should not be done enough! Suppose it should break in turning out! Suppose somebody should have got over the wall of the back-yard, and stolen it, while they were merry with the goose—a supposition at which the two young Cratchits became livid! All sorts of horrors were supposed.

Halloa! A great deal of steam! The pudding was out of the copper. A smell like a washing-day! That was the cloth. A smell like an eating-house and a pastry-cook's next door to each other, with a laundress's next door to that! That was the pudding! In half a minute Mrs. Cratchit entered—flushed, but smiling proudly—with the pudding, like a speckled cannon-ball, so hard and firm, blazing in half of half a quartern of ignited brandy, and bedight with Christmas holly stuck into the top.

Oh, a wonderful pudding! Bob Cratchit said, and calmly too, that he regarded it as the greatest success achieved by Mrs. Cratchit since their marriage. Mrs. Cratchit said that now the weight was off her mind, she would confess she had had her doubts about the quantity of flour. Everybody had something to say about it, but nobody said or thought it was at all a small pudding for a large family. It would have been flat heresy to do so. Any Cratchit would have blushed to hint at such a thing.

At last the dinner was all done, the cloth was cleared, the hearth swept, and the fire made up. The compound in the jug being tasted, and considered perfect, apples and oranges were put upon the table, and a shovelful of chestnuts on the fire. Then all the Cratchit family drew round the hearth in what Bob Cratchit called a circle, meaning half a one; and at Bob Cratchit's elbow stood the family display of glass. Two tumblers, and a custard-cup without a handle.

These held the hot stuff from the jug, however, as well as golden goblets would have done; and Bob served it out with beaming looks, while the chestnuts on the fire sputtered and cracked noisily. Then Bob proposed:

"A Merry Christmas to us all, my dears. God bless us!"

Which all the family re-echoed.

"God bless us every one!" said Tiny Tim, the last of all.

from *A Christmas Carol*

IN THE BLEAK MID-WINTER

1 In the bleak mid-winter,
　Frosty wind made moan,
Earth stood hard as iron,
　Water like a stone;
Snow had fallen, snow on snow,
　Snow on snow,
In the bleak mid-winter,
　Long ago.

2 Our God, Heaven cannot hold Him
　Nor earth sustain;
Heaven and earth shall flee away
　When He comes to reign.
In the bleak mid-winter
　A stable-place sufficed
The Lord God Almighty
　Jesus Christ.

3 Enough for Him, whom cherubim
　Worship night and day,
A breastful of milk
　And a mangerful of hay;
Enough for Him whom angels
　Fall down before,
The ox and ass and camel
　Which adore.

4 Angels and archangels
　May have gathered there,
Cherubim and seraphim
　Throng'd the air,
But only His mother
　In her maiden bliss
Worshipped the Beloved
　With a kiss.

5 What can I give Him,
　Poor as I am?
If I were a shepherd
　I would bring a lamb,
If I were a wise man
　I would do my part—
Yet what I can I give Him,
　Give my heart.

Christina Rossetti

SAINT NICHOLAS

NORA CLARKE

Saint Nicholas is thought to have lived in Asia Minor over fifteen hundred years ago. He was a Christian priest and later became a bishop. Nicholas traveled all over the country helping people; he was rich and gave away gifts of money and other presents. Nicholas was a modest man who never boasted about his generosity but preferred to keep it secret.

One tale about Saint Nicholas is that he was once staying in an inn where three young boys had been murdered and their bodies hidden in a barrel of pickles. By some miracle, Nicholas is said to have breathed life into all the boys. Perhaps it is as a result of this that he became known as a children's saint. It is certainly true that the tradition developed that boys and girls were given small presents of fruit and sweets on Nicholas's feast day, December 6. Parents would ask their children to leave hay, straw, or even a carrot outside for the saint's horse. They reminded children that Nicholas did not like to be seen when he gave away presents, so they had to go to sleep quickly or he would not come!

Another story about Saint Nicholas is that he once heard of a poor man who had no money to give his three daughters on their wedding day. The generous bishop secretly dropped bags of gold down the chimney of their house and these fell into the stockings which the girls had left to dry by the fire. The sisters found the gold and, ever since, children have hung up stockings on Christmas Eve hoping that they will be filled with presents by morning.

Bishop Nicholas was declared a saint after his death. Today many people know him as Santa Claus; this name comes from the Dutch for Saint Nicholas, Sinter Klaas. He is also known as Father Christmas.

A VISIT FROM ST. NICHOLAS

'Twas the night before Christmas, when all through
                  the house
Not a creature was stirring, not even a mouse;
The stockings were hung by the chimney with care,
In hopes that St. Nicholas soon would be there;
The children were nestled all snug in their beds,
While visions of sugar-plums danced in their heads;
And mamma in her 'kerchief, and I in my cap,
Had just settled our brains for a long winter's nap;
When out on the lawn there arose such a clatter,
I sprang from the bed to see what was the matter.
Away to the window I flew like a flash,
Tore open the shutters and threw up the sash.
The moon on the breast of the new-fallen snow,
Gave the lustre of mid-day to objects below,
When, what to my wondering eyes should appear,
But a miniature sleigh, and eight tiny reindeer,
With a little old driver, so lively and quick,
I knew in a moment it must be St. Nick.
More rapid than eagles his coursers they came,
And he whistled and shouted, and called them by name;
"Now, *Dasher*! now, *Dancer*! now, *Prancer* and *Vixen*!
On, *Comet*! on, *Cupid*! on, *Donder* and *Blitzen*!
To the top of the porch! to the top of the wall!
Now dash away! dash away! dash away all!"
As dry leaves that before the wild hurricane fly,
When they meet with an obstacle, mount to the sky,
So up to the house-top the coursers they flew,

With the sleigh full of toys, and St. Nicholas too.
And then, in a twinkling, I heard on the roof
The prancing and pawing of each little hoof.
As I drew in my head, and was turning around,
Down the chimney St. Nicholas came with a bound.
He was dressed all in fur, from his head to his foot,
And his clothes were all tarnished with ashes and soot;
A bundle of toys he had flung on his back,
And he looked like a peddler just opening his pack.
His eyes—how they twinkled! his dimples, how merry!
His cheeks were like roses, his nose like a cherry!
His droll little mouth was drawn up like a bow,
And the beard of his chin was as white as the snow;
The stump of a pipe he held tight in his teeth,
And the smoke it encircled his head like a wreath;
He had a broad face and a little round belly,
That shook, when he laughed, like a bowl full of jelly.
He was chubby and plump, a right jolly old elf,
And I laughed when I saw him, in spite of myself;
A wink of his eye and a twist of his head,
Soon gave me to know I had nothing to dread;
He spoke not a word, but went straight to his work,
And filled all the stockings; then turned with a jerk,
And laying his finger aside of his nose,
And giving a nod, up the chimney he rose;
He sprang to his sleigh, to his team gave a whistle,
And away they all flew like the down of a thistle.
But I heard him exclaim, ere he drove out of sight,
"Happy Christmas to all, and to all a good night."

Clement C. Moore

O COME, ALL YE FAITHFUL

English Carol

O come, all ye faith - ful, Joy - ful and tri - um - phant, O
come ye, O come___ ye to Beth - le - hem;
Come and be - hold Him; Born the King of an - gels; O
come, let us a - dore Him, O come, let us a - dore Him, O
come, let us a - dore Him, ___ Christ ___ the Lord.

CHORUS

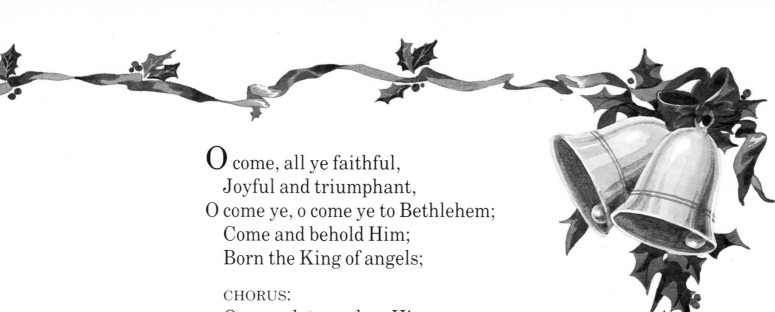

O come, all ye faithful,
   Joyful and triumphant,
O come ye, o come ye to Bethlehem;
   Come and behold Him;
   Born the King of angels;

CHORUS:
   O come, let us adore Him,
   O come, let us adore Him,
   O come, let us adore Him,
   Christ the Lord:

God of God,
   Light of Light,
Lo! He abhors not the Virgin's womb;
   Very God,
   Begotten, not created;

   CHORUS

Sing, choirs of angels,
   Sing in exultation,
O sing, all ye citizens of heav'n above;
   Glory to God
   In the highest.

   CHORUS

Yea, Lord, we greet Thee,
   Born this happy morning,
Jesu, to Thee be glory giv'n;
   Word of the Father,
   Now in flesh appearing;

   CHORUS

CHRISTMAS AT MOLE END

KENNETH GRAHAME

What a capital little house this is!" Mr. Rat called out cheerily. "So compact! So well planned! Everything here and everything in its place! We'll make a jolly night of it. The first thing we want is a good fire; I'll see to that—I always know where to find things. So this is the parlour? Splendid! Your own idea, those little sleeping-bunks in the wall? Capital! Now, I'll fetch the wood and the coals, and you get a duster, Mole—you'll find one in the drawer of the kitchen table—and try and smarten things up a bit. Bustle about, old chap!"

Encouraged by his inspiriting companion, the Mole roused himself and dusted and polished with energy and heartiness, while the Rat, running to and fro with armfuls of fuel, soon had a cheerful blaze roaring up the chimney. He hailed the Mole to come and warm himself; but Mole promptly had another fit of the blues, dropping down on a couch in dark despair and burying his face in his duster.

"Rat," he moaned, "how about your supper, you poor, cold, hungry, weary animal? I've nothing to give you—nothing—not a crumb!"

"What a fellow you are for giving in!" said the Rat reproachfully. "Why, only just now I saw a sardine-opener on the kitchen dresser, quite distinctly; and everybody knows that means there are sardines about somewhere in the neighbourhood. Rouse yourself! pull yourself together, and come with me and forage."

They went and foraged accordingly, hunting through every cupboard and turning out every drawer. The result was not so very depressing after all, though of course it might have been better; a tin of sardines—a box of captain's biscuits, nearly full—and a German sausage encased in silver paper.

"There's a banquet for you!" observed the Rat, as he arranged the table. "I know some animals who would give their ears to be sitting down to supper with us tonight!"

"No bread!" groaned the Mole dolorously; "no butter, no—"

"No *pâté de foie gras*, no champagne!" continued the Rat, grinning. "And that reminds me—what's that little door at the end of the passage? Your cellar, of course! Every luxury in this house! Just you wait a minute."

He made for the cellar door, and presently re-appeared, somewhat dusty, with a bottle of beer in each paw and another under each arm. "Self-indulgent beggar you seem to be, Mole," he observed. "Deny yourself nothing. This is really the jolliest little place I ever was in. Now, wherever did you pick up those prints? Make the place look so home-like, they do. No wonder you're so fond of it, Mole. Tell us all about it, and how you came to make it what it is."

Then, while the Rat busied himself fetching plates, and knives and forks, and mustard which he mixed in an egg-cup, the Mole, his bosom still heaving with the stress of his recent emotion, related—somewhat shyly at first, but with more freedom as he warmed to his subject—how this was planned, and how that was thought out, and how this was got through a windfall from an aunt, and that was a wonderful find and a bargain, and this other thing was bought out of laborious savings and a certain amount of "going without." His spirits finally quite restored, he must needs go and caress his possessions, and take a lamp and show off their points to his visitor, and expatiate on them, quite forgetful of the supper they both so much needed; Rat, who was desperately hungry but strove to conceal it, nodding seriously, examining with a puckered brow, and saying "Wonderful," and "Most remarkable," at intervals, when the chance for an observation was given him.

At last the Rat succeeded in decoying him to the table, and had just got seriously to work with the sardine-opener when sounds were heard from the forecourt without—sounds like the scuffling of small feet in the gravel and a confused murmur of tiny voices, while broken sentences reached them— "Now, all in a line—hold the lantern up a bit, Tommy—clear your throats first—no coughing after I say one, two, three.—Where's young Bill?—Here, come on, do, we're all a-waiting—"

"What's up?" inquired the Rat, pausing in his labours.

"I think it must be the field-mice," replied the Mole, with a touch of pride in his manner. "They go round carol-singing regularly at this time of the year. They're quite an institution in these parts. And they never pass me over— they come to Mole End last of all; and I used to give them hot drinks, and supper too sometimes, when I could afford it. It will be like old times to hear them again."

"Let's have a look!" cried the Rat, jumping up and running to the door.

It was a pretty sight, and a seasonable one, that met their eyes when they flung the door open. In the forecourt, lit by the dim rays of a horn lantern, some eight or ten little field-mice stood in a semicircle, red worsted comforters round their throats, their fore-paws thrust deep into their pockets, their feet jigging for warmth. With bright beady eyes they glanced shyly at each other, sniggering a little, sniffing and applying coat-sleeves a good deal. As the door opened, one of the elder ones that carried the lantern was just saying, "Now then, one, two, three!" and forthwith their shrill little voices uprose on the air, singing one of the old-time carols that their forefathers composed in fields that were fallow and held by frost, or when snow-bound in chimney corners, and handed down to be sung in the miry street to lamp-lit windows.

CAROL
Villagers all, this frosty tide,
Let your doors swing open wide,
Though wind may follow, and snow beside,
Yet draw us in by your fire to bide;
    Joy shall be yours in the morning!

Here we stand in the cold and the sleet,
Blowing fingers and stamping feet,
Come from far away you to greet—
You by the fire and we in the street—
    Bidding you joy in the morning!

For ere one half of the night was gone,
Sudden a star has led us on,
Raining bliss and benison—
Bliss tomorrow and more anon,
    Joy for every morning!

Goodman Joseph toiled through the snow—
Saw the star o'er a stable low;
Mary she might not further go—
Welcome thatch, and litter below!
    Joy was hers in the morning.

And then they heard the angels tell
"Who were the first to cry Nowell?
Animals all, as it befell,
In the stable where they did dwell!
    Joy shall be theirs in the morning!"

The voices ceased, the singers, bashful but smiling, exchanged sidelong glances, and silence succeeded—but for a moment only. Then, from up above and far away, down the tunnel they had so lately traveled was borne to their ears in a faint musical hum the sound of distant bells ringing a joyful and clangorous peal.

"Very well sung, boys!" cried the Rat heartily. "And now come along in, all of you, and warm yourselves by the fire, and have something hot!"

"Yes, come along, field mice," cried the Mole eagerly. "This is quite like old times! Shut the door after you. Pull up that settle to the fire. Now, you just wait a minute, while we—O, Ratty!" he cried in despair, plumping down on a seat, with tears impending. "Whatever are we doing? We've nothing to give them!"

"You leave all that to me," said the masterful Rat. "Here, you with the lantern! Come over this way. I want to talk to you. Now, tell me, are there any shops open at this hour of the night?"

"Why, certainly, sir," replied the field-mouse respectfully. "At this time of the year our shops keep open to all sorts of hours."

"Then look here!" said the Rat. "You go off at once, you and your lantern, and you get me—"

Here much muttered conversation ensued, and the Mole only heard bits of it, such as—"Fresh, mind!—no, a pound of that will do—see you get Buggins's, for I won't have any other—no, only the best—if you can't get it there, try somewhere else—yes, of course, home-made, no tinned stuff—well then, do the best you can!" Finally, there was a chink of coin passing from paw to paw, the field-mouse was provided with an ample basket for his purchases, and off he hurried, he and his lantern.

The rest of the field-mice, perched in a row on the settle, their small legs swinging, gave themselves up to the enjoyment of the fire, and toasted their chilblains till they tingled; while the Mole, failing to draw them into easy conversation, plunged into family history and made each of them recite the names of his numerous brothers, who were too young, it appeared, to be allowed to go out a-carolling this year, but looked forward very shortly to winning the parental consent.

The Rat, meanwhile, was busy examining the label on one of the beer-bottles. "I perceive this to be Old Burton," he remarked approvingly. "*Sensible* Mole! The very thing! Now we shall be able to mull some ale! Get the things ready, Mole, while I draw the corks."

It did not take long to prepare the brew and thrust the tin heater well into the red heart of the fire; and soon every field-mouse was sipping and coughing and choking (for a little mulled ale goes a long way) and wiping his eyes and laughing and forgetting he had ever been cold in all his life.

"They act plays too, these fellows," the Mole explained to the Rat. "Make them up all by themselves, and act them afterwards. And very well they do it, too! They gave us a capital one last year, about a field-mouse who was captured at sea by a Barbary corsair, and made to row in a galley; and when he escaped and got home again, his lady-love had gone into a convent. Here, *you!* You were in it, I remember. Get up and recite a bit."

The field-mouse addressed got up on his legs, giggled shyly, looked round the room, and remained absolutely tongue-tied. His comrades cheered him on, Mole coaxed and encouraged him, and the Rat went so far as to take him by the shoulders and shake him; but nothing could overcome his stage-fright. They were all busily engaged on him like watermen applying the Royal Humane Society's regulations to a case of long submersion, when the latch clicked, the door opened, and the field-mouse with the lantern reappeared, staggering under the weight of his basket.

There was no more talk of play-acting once the very real and solid contents of the basket had been tumbled out on the table. Under the generalship of Rat, everybody was set to do something or to fetch something. In a very few minutes supper was ready, and Mole, as he took the head of the table in a sort of dream, saw a lately barren board set thick with savoury comforts; saw his little friends' faces brighten and beam as they fell to without delay; and then let himself loose—for he was famished indeed—on the provender so magically provided, thinking what a happy home-coming this had turned out, after all. As they ate, they talked of old times, and the field-mice gave him the local gossip up to date, and answered as well as they could the hundred questions he had to ask them. The Rat said little or nothing, only taking care that each guest had what he wanted, and plenty of it, and that Mole had no trouble or anxiety about anything.

They clattered off at last, very grateful and showering wishes of the season, with their jacket pockets stuffed with remembrances for the small brothers and sisters at home. When the door had closed on the last of them and the chink of the lanterns had died away, Mole and Rat kicked the fire up, drew their chairs in, brewed themselves a last nightcap of mulled ale, and discussed the events of the long day. At last the Rat, with a tremendous yawn, said, "Mole, old chap, I'm ready to drop. Sleepy is simply not the word. That your own bunk over on that side? Very well, then, I'll take this. What a ripping little house this is! Everything so handy!"

He clambered into his bunk and rolled himself well up in the blankets, and slumber gathered him forthwith, as a swath of barley is folded into the arms of the reaping-machine.

The weary Mole also was glad to turn in without delay, and soon had his head on his pillow, in great joy and contentment. But ere he closed his eyes he let them wander round his old room, mellow in the glow of the firelight that played or rested on familiar and friendly things which had long been unconsciously a part of him, and now smilingly received him back, without rancour. He was now in just the frame of mind that the tactful Rat had quietly worked to bring about in him. He saw clearly how plain and simple—how narrow, even—it all was; but clearly, too, how much it all meant to him, and the special value of some such anchorage in one's existence. He did not at all want to abandon the new life and its splendid spaces, to turn his back on sun and air and all they offered him and creep home and stay there; the upper world was all too strong, it called to him still, even down there, and he knew he must return to the larger stage. But it was good to think he had this to come back to, this place which was all his own, these things which were so glad to see him again and could always be counted upon for the same simple welcome.

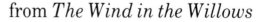

from *The Wind in the Willows*

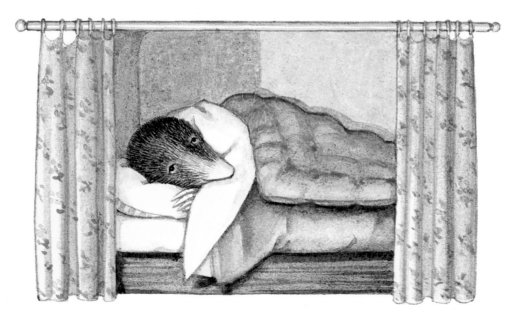

JOURNEY OF THE MAGI

"A cold coming we had of it,
Just the worst time of the year
For a journey, and such a long journey:
The ways deep and the weather sharp,
The very dead of winter."
And the camels galled, sore-footed, refractory,
Lying down in the melting snow.
There were times we regretted
The summer palaces on slopes, the terraces,
And the silken girls bringing sherbet.
Then the camel men cursing and grumbling
And running away, and wanting their liquor and women,
And the night-fires going out, and the lack of shelters,
And the cities hostile and the towns unfriendly
And the villages dirty and charging high prices:
A hard time we had of it.
At the end we preferred to travel all night,
Sleeping in snatches,
With the voices singing in our ears, saying
That this was all folly.

Then at dawn we came down to a temperate valley,
Wet, below the snow line, smelling of vegetation,
With a running stream and a water-mill beating the darkness,
And three trees on the low sky.
And an old white horse galloped away in the meadow.
Then we came to a tavern with vine-leaves over the lintel,
Six hands at an open door dicing for pieces of silver,
And feet kicking the empty wine-skins.
But there was no information, and so we continued
And arrived at evening, not a moment too soon
Finding the place; it was (you may say) satisfactory.

All this was a long time ago, I remember,
And I would do it again, but set down
This set down
This: were we led all that way for
Birth or Death? There was a Birth, certainly,
We had evidence and no doubt. I had seen birth and death,
But had thought they were different; this Birth was
Hard and bitter agony for us, like Death, our death.
We returned to our places, these Kingdoms,
But no longer at ease here, in the old dispensation,
With an alien people clutching their gods.
I should be glad of another death.

T. S. Eliot

AWAY IN A MANGER

English Carol

Away in a manger, no crib for a bed,
The little Lord Jesus laid down His sweet head.
The stars in the bright sky looked down where He lay:
The little Lord Jesus asleep on the hay.

The cattle are lowing, the baby awakes,
But little Lord Jesus no crying He makes.
I love Thee, Lord Jesus! Look down from the sky,
And stay by my side until morning is nigh.

Be near me, Lord Jesus; I ask Thee to stay
Close by me for ever, and love me, I pray.
Bless all the dear children in Thy tender care,
And fit us for heaven, to live with Thee there.

SILENT NIGHT
German Carol

Silent night, holy night,
   All is calm, all is bright
Round yon Virgin Mother and Child,
   Holy infant so tender and mild.
Sleep in heavenly peace,
Sleep in heavenly peace.

Silent night, holy night,
   Darkness flies, all is light.
Shepherds hear the angels sing,
   "Alleluia, hail the King!"
Jesus the Saviour is born,
Jesus the Saviour is born.

Silent night, holy night,
   Wondrous star, lend thy light:
With the angels let us sing
   Alleluia to our king.
Christ the Saviour is born,
Christ the Saviour is born.

Joseph Mohr

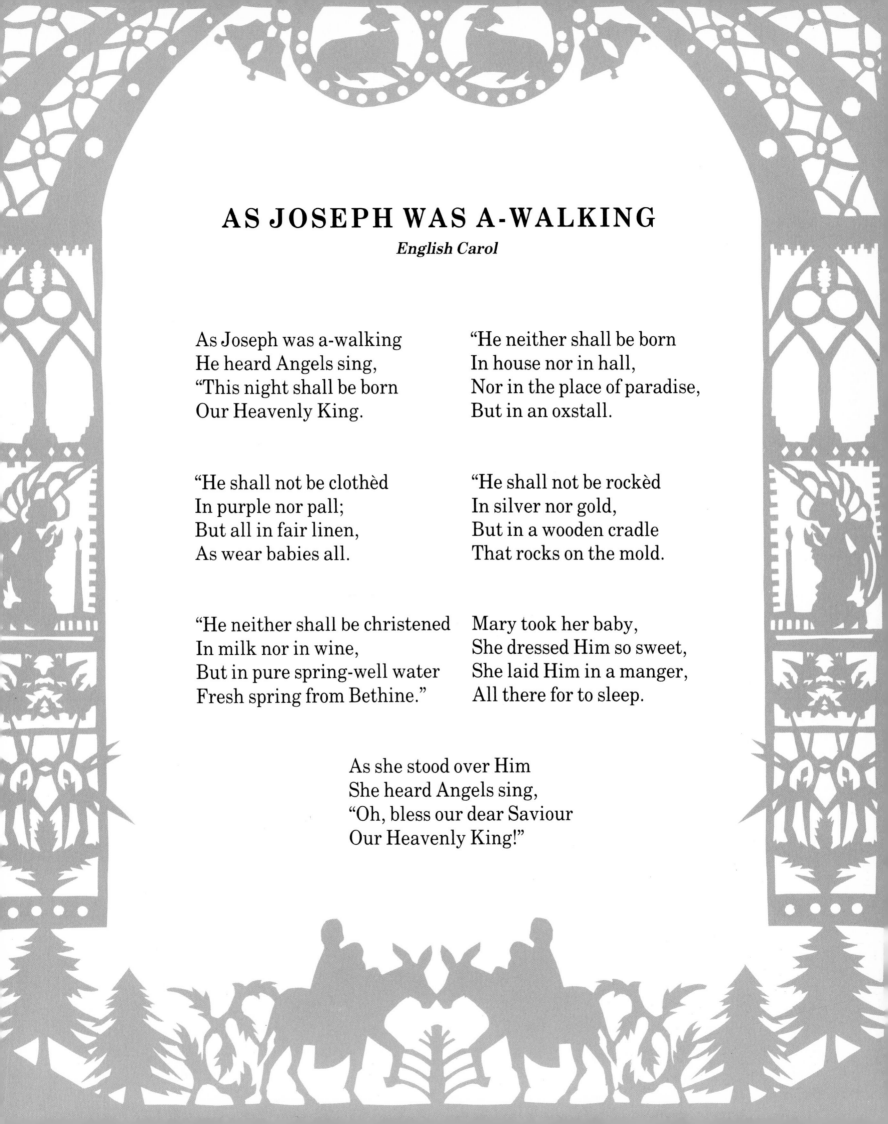

AS JOSEPH WAS A-WALKING

English Carol

As Joseph was a-walking
He heard Angels sing,
"This night shall be born
Our Heavenly King.

"He shall not be clothèd
In purple nor pall;
But all in fair linen,
As wear babies all.

"He neither shall be christened
In milk nor in wine,
But in pure spring-well water
Fresh spring from Bethine."

"He neither shall be born
In house nor in hall,
Nor in the place of paradise,
But in an oxstall.

"He shall not be rockèd
In silver nor gold,
But in a wooden cradle
That rocks on the mold.

Mary took her baby,
She dressed Him so sweet,
She laid Him in a manger,
All there for to sleep.

As she stood over Him
She heard Angels sing,
"Oh, bless our dear Saviour
Our Heavenly King!"

CELEBRATING CHRISTMAS

NORA CLARKE

In the United States and in Britain, Santa Claus arrives for Christmas in a sleigh drawn by reindeer with tinkling bells on their harness. He has a bushy white beard and wears a long red robe. However, in other countries there are different ways of welcoming Christmas, many of which do not include a visit from Santa Claus.

In Holland, December 6 is the special day of St. Nicholas, the children's saint. His Dutch name is Sinter Klaus, and he arrives with his servant Black Peter, riding on a beautiful white horse. Dutch children believe that Black Peter keeps notes about their behavior in a big book. On December 6, good children will be given presents, and he will chase the naughty ones with a big stick.

Tradition has it that St. Nicholas rides over the rooftops, so children leave stockings or clogs by the fireplace filled with carrots and hay. They hope that he will take these for his horse and leave presents for them.

In Italy, France, and Spain, fireworks are set off on Christmas Night, and Père Noël visits French children and leaves presents in their *sabots*. Many French families leave a glowing fire, burning candles, and food nearby as a reminder of the weary travelers Mary and Joseph so long ago.

Italian children receive their gifts on January 6, Epiphany, which is traditionally the time the Wise Men brought their gifts to Bethlehem. Mexican children also receive presents on January 6, but they prepare for Christmas on December 16 when they dress up for a procession called a *posada*, the Spanish word for "inn." They carry candles and a board with figures of Mary and Joseph on it. They sing carols outside houses asking for shelter for the travelers.

"No room at the inn," they are told, so they go on until they find a *posada* which welcomes them. They do this nine times. By the last procession on Christmas Eve, they have added a stable, a manger, and small animals to the board. Then, at midnight, the last model, which is of Baby Jesus, is added.

Next, children and grown-ups take gifts to church which are given away later. There is a story which tells of a little Mexican girl long ago who was so poor that she had nothing to take to the crib. Sad and lonely, she stood watching the procession, then she turned away into the churchyard where she saw an

angel carved in stone. Tall grasses and weeds almost covered the face, so she knelt to clear some away. Suddenly she heard a voice.

"Pick these weeds," she heard it say. "Take them to the church and offer them to the Christ-child."

The little girl picked an armful of weeds, then she walked rather fearfully into the church and went toward the crib. As she went, the top of each weed turned bright red like a tip of fire. Ever since people have grown these plants specially for Christmas. They are called "poinsettias," but their other name is "Fire Flowers of the Holy Night."

In countries like Sweden, Norway, Finland, and Poland animals may starve in the freezing winter conditions, so children there begin their Christmas celebrations by putting out extra food for them. Farmers often hang a sheaf of grain in the trees, and in Sweden a little elf called Nisse is given a small bowl of porridge to make sure he guards the farm animals well.

St. Lucia's Day begins the Christmas season for Swedish children. It is said that early Christians were often ill-treated so they hid in dark secret caves. St. Lucia was a very brave young girl who took food to these refugees at night. She did not worry about the dangers, but wore a crown of candles so that she could carry more things and still see her path in the dark. In the end she was caught and killed, so on December 13 the youngest girl in the family or school wears a long white dress and a crown of evergreens and candles. She carries a tray of gingerbread and special Lucia buns to her parents, schoolfriends, or to sick people, in memory of Lucia.

In India, where it is very hot, banana and mango trees are decorated. Christian children follow the Hindu festival of Light custom and put small glowing lamps around the edges of balconies and flat roofs.

Australian children may have Christmas dinner on the beach, with barbecued turkey and plum pudding ice cream, but in whatever different ways we celebrate Christmas, they are all ways of remembering the birth of Christ in Bethlehem almost two thousand years ago.

FROHLICHE WEIHNACHTEN
MERRY CHRISTMAS
BUON NATALE
JOYEUX NOEL
ALIG KERSTFEEST

GOOD KING WENCESLAS

English Carol

Good King Wenceslas looked out
  On the feast of Stephen,
When the snow lay round about,
  Deep and crisp and even;
Brightly shone the moon that night,
  Though the frost was cruel,
When a poor man came in sight,
  Gathering winter fuel.

"Hither, page, and stand by me,
  If thou know'st it, telling,
Yonder peasant, who is he?
  Where and what his dwelling?"
"Sire, he lives a good league hence,
  Underneath the mountain,
Right against the forest fence,
  By Saint Agnes' fountain."

"Bring me flesh and bring me wine,
	Bring me pine logs hither;
Thou and I will see him dine,
	When we bear them thither."
Page and monarch forth they went,
	Forth they went together,
Through the rude wind's wild lament
	And the bitter weather.

"Sire, the night is darker now,
	And the wind blows stronger;
Fails my heart, I know not how,
	I can go no longer."
"Mark my footsteps, good my page!
	Tread thou in them boldly:
Thou shalt find the winter's rage
	Freeze thy blood less coldly."

In his master's steps he trod,
	Where the snow lay dinted;
Heat was in the very sod
	Which the saint had printed.
Therefore, Christian men, be sure,
	Wealth or rank possessing,
Ye who now will bless the poor,
	Shall yourselves find blessing.

THE ELVES AND THE SHOEMAKER

THE BROTHERS GRIMM

Once upon a time there lived a poor shoemaker. He made very good shoes and worked very hard, but he still could not earn enough money for himself and his family. At last he became so poor that he could not even afford to buy the leather to make the shoes. In the end he had only enough leather to make one last pair. He cut them out very carefully and put the pieces on his workbench ready for sewing the next morning.

"I wonder if I'll ever make another pair of shoes after these," he sighed. "When I've sold this last pair I shall need all the money to buy food for my family. There will be nothing to spare for new leather."

He went to bed that night a sad and troubled man.

Next morning the shoemaker got up early and went down to his workshop. There, on the bench, he found a beautiful pair of shoes! The stitches were tiny and even, and so perfectly formed that he knew he could never have made a better pair himself. When he looked more closely, he realized that they were made from the leather pieces which he had laid out the night before. Quickly he put the fine pair of shoes in the window of his shop and drew back the blinds.

"Who could have done this for me?" he wondered. But before he could think of an answer, a grand gentleman came in and bought the shoes. He willingly paid a much higher price than usual. The delighted shoemaker immediately went out and bought plenty of food and more leather. This time he cut out two pairs of shoes and laid all the pieces on his bench ready for sewing the next day. Then he closed the shop and went upstairs to have a good supper with his family.

"Goodness gracious!" he exclaimed the following day when he found two pairs of beautifully finished shoes on his workbench. "How can anyone make shoes so well and so quickly too?" He put them in his shop window, and before long some rich people came in and paid a lot of money for them. The shoemaker was very happy. He went straight out and bought some more leather to cut out more shoes.

This went on for weeks, and then months. Sometimes the shoemaker cut

two pairs, sometimes four pairs, but they were always finished by morning. The little shop was crowded with customers as people told each other about the shoemaker's excellent shoes. He cut out many different kinds: sturdy fur-lined boots, delicate dancing slippers, ladies' walking shoes, children's shoes, shoes with laces, shoes with bows, and shoes with silver buckles. He prospered and even became quite a rich man. His wife and children were happy.

"I wish I knew who was helping us," he said to his wife one evening as they chatted by the fire.

"Why don't we hide behind that cupboard in the workroom," she suggested, "then we'll find out who our kind, hard-working helpers are."

So they did just that, and as the clock struck midnight they heard a bustling, rustling noise. Two little men were squeezing through a crack under the door. They each carried a bag of tools. But the strangest thing was that they wore no clothes at all. They perched on the workbench and started work. Their tiny hands stitched and their little hammers tapped without a moment's pause.

"How can they make so many beautiful shoes so quickly when they are so small?" whispered the shoemaker. For truly the elves were no bigger than his own needles.

"Ssssh," his wife replied. "Look, they're tidying up."

At that moment the elves disappeared under the door.

"The little elves have helped us so much," the shoemaker's wife said thoughtfully the next day. "As Christmas is almost here why don't we make some presents for them?"

"What a splendid idea!" the shoemaker cried. "I'll make some tiny boots, if you'll make them some clothes."

So husband and wife stitched away late into the night and much of the next day. On Christmas Eve their gifts were ready, and they laid them out on the workbench. There were two little green jackets and two pairs of trousers, and two little woolen caps to match. They also put out a plate of small cakes and cookies, and two little glasses of wine. Then they hid behind the cupboard again and kept watch.

At midnight the little elves appeared. They jumped onto the bench to begin work, but then they saw all the little presents. With excited shouts they put on the jackets, the little trousers, the woolly caps, and the fine leather boots. Then they spied the food and the wine and they laughed with delight as they ate and drank everything that had been put out for them. After that, the little

elves hopped down from the bench, danced merrily around the workroom, then disappeared under the doorway.

After Christmas, the shoemaker cut out his leather as usual, but the elves never came back to his workroom.

"Perhaps they heard us whispering," his wife suggested. "Elves are very shy of human folk."

"Well, I shall miss their kind help," declared her husband, "but my shop is busy now, and always crowded with customers. I daresay we shall manage without them, even though my stitches will never be as fine as theirs."

The shoemaker and his family did indeed continue to prosper, but they never forgot the kind elves who had helped them so much when times were hard. Every Christmas Eve they would fill their glasses around the fire and drink a toast to their little friends.

MARY'S SONG

Sleep, King Jesus,
Your royal bed
Is made of hay
In a cattle-shed.
Sleep, King Jesus,
Do not fear,
Joseph is watching
And waiting near.

Warm in the wintry air
You lie,
The ox and the donkey
Standing by,
With summer eyes
They seem to say:
Welcome, Jesus,
On Christmas Day!

Sleep, King Jesus:
Your diamond crown
High in the sky
Where the stars look down.
Let your reign
Of love begin,
That all the world
May enter in.

Charles Causley